Time Management

Enhancing Time Management Skills For Students:
Empowering Students: A Practical Manual For Achieving
Academic Excellence And Overall Development

(Analysing And Assessing Your Time Management)

Lester Campbell

TABLE OF CONTNET

Handling The Procrastination Issue 1

Managing Time At Work 6

Making A Successful Timetable 12

How To Put The Pomodoro Technique Into Practice 26

The Merger And Acquisition Of 46

Time-Management Strategies 67

Establishing A Habit Of Time Management 78

Monitor Your Development And Honour Victories 105

Benefits Of Effective Time Management. 116

Setting Goals Is Crucial For Any Organisation. 127

Handling The Procrastination Issue

Knowing Why People Procrastinate

One prevalent issue that impairs productivity and time management is procrastination.

This chapter will examine the reasons behind procrastination as well as practical solutions.

Finding the Reasons Behind Procrastination

The root reasons for procrastination must be found to counteract it.

The following are a few typical causes:

Fear of Not Getting Enough Done Procrastination might be caused by a fear of making mistakes or failing to achieve the intended goals.

Overcoming this obstacle requires acknowledging and confronting these fears.

Absence of drive: We are more prone to put things off when we lack sufficient motivation.

Overcoming this obstacle can be facilitated by identifying your motivational factors and developing strategies to enhance them.

Discouraging Tasks: Procrastination commonly responds to tedious, challenging, or unpleasant jobs.

To prevent procrastinating, it is essential to learn how to manage these responsibilities well.

Techniques for Overcoming Procrastination

Let's now examine some practical methods for beating procrastination:

Split Up the Work: Divide more difficult, larger jobs into smaller, more doable segments.

As a result, the task appears less intimidating and is more manageable.

Set deadlines: Give your assignments reasonable due dates and commit to meeting them.

Setting deadlines gives you focus and a sense of urgency that prevents you from putting things off.

Employ Time Management Strategies: working in concentrated bursts separated by relaxation times.

This aids in maintaining concentration and boosting output.

Determine When You're Most Productive: Decide when you are most alert and invigorated during the day, and save that period for the most significant and difficult assignments.

You can prevent procrastination by making the most of your highest production level.

Developing Productive Routines

It is critical to develop productive habits to overcome procrastination over time.

The following are some practical tactics:

Includes time set aside for priorities and significant tasks.

Establishing and adhering to a routine fosters discipline and prevents procrastination.

Take Away Distractions: Determine which distractions can cause you to put things off and eliminate them.

Close unnecessary tabs in your browser, turn off your phone's notifications and arrange your workspace to be distraction-free.

Develop Your "No" Skills: Learn to say "no" to things and requests that don't fit your priorities.

This helps you avoid work overload and concentrate on what is important.

Apply Self-Compassion to Combat Procrastination

Although overcoming procrastination can be difficult, it's critical to remember to practise self-compassion.

Here are some pointers:

Don't Be Hard on Yourself: Refrain from blaming or harshly criticising yourself for your delay.

Rather, acknowledge that it's a typical occurrence and concentrate on developing constructive fixes.

Honour minor victories: Acknowledge and congratulate every work and step that has been performed.

This strengthens a feeling of accomplishment and provides encouragement to keep going.

Ask for Help: If you're having trouble stopping yourself from doing something, you might want to talk to friends, family, or a coach.

Having a support system and someone to keep you responsible can help.

I hope you now understand procrastination better and how it might affect your time management after reading this chapter.

Procrastination may be identified and dealt with skillfully, which will help you become more productive and efficient with your time.

In the upcoming chapters, we'll look at methods and approaches for beating procrastination and developing more productive habits.

Get ready to overcome procrastination and accomplish significant outcomes.

Managing Time At Work

The value of time management in the workplace

Successful and productive time management is essential for success in the workplace.

This chapter will cover methods and approaches for increasing productivity and making the most use of your time at work.

Setting Priorities

Establishing your priorities is a crucial first step in time management at work.

Here are some pointers to assist you:

Evaluate the tasks:

Examine your tasks and decide which are most essential and crucial.

Give these chores top priority and provide enough time to finish them.

Establish Daily Objectives: Establish specific daily objectives to direct your work efforts.

You'll be able to maintain focus and concentrate your efforts on the things that count.

Time-Management Strategies in the Workplace

You can use several efficient time management strategies in the office.

These are a handful of the most well-liked ones:

The Pomodoro Method: Employ the Pomodoro approach, which has you working in concentrated intervals—typically 25 minutes—interspersed with quick breaks for recovery.

This method aids in preserving focus and preventing fatigue.

Assigning work that other team members can complete is a good idea.

By doing this, you may divide the workload and concentrate on more important things.

Email management: Instead of being interrupted by emails all the time, set up specific times to check and reply to them.

Use folders or tags to organize your email to maintain a more productive workflow.

Steer clear of excessive multitasking: Attempting to accomplish too many tasks at once may be appealing, but doing so frequently leads to decreased productivity.

Concentrate on one activity at a time, finishing it before going on to the next.

Removing Diversions

Distractions at work have the potential to seriously impair time management.

Here are some strategies to reduce distractions and boost productivity: Disable Notifications: Disable notifications from mobile apps and devices that can interfere with your work.

This will allow you to work on projects without being constantly distracted.

Establish a Focused Workplace: Set up your workspace to reduce outside distractions.

Keep your space neat and orderly, and eliminate anything extra that could divert your attention.

Establish Time Boundaries for Talks and Interruptions: Use assertiveness when establishing time limitations for discussions and social contacts at work.

This keeps you from getting sidetracked and demonstrates to coworkers that you are committed to your work.

Managing Time in Teams and Projects

It's critical to plan and work with teams and projects and manage your time.

The following are some methods for efficiently managing team time:

Unambiguous Communication: Create effective and transparent communication channels to promote cooperation and information exchange.

What is meant by realistic deadlines? Establish reasonable timelines for tasks and projects when working as a team, keeping in mind the team's capabilities and the availability of resources.

Effective Gatherings: Establish a defined agenda and a time limit to help you run well-organized and productive meetings.

Ensure that every conversation advances the project and is pertinent.

By putting particular tactics into practice to handle workloads and increase productivity, you'll build strong groundwork for obtaining significant outcomes.

The following chapters will cover strategies for improving time management on a personal level and striking a healthy balance between work and personal life.

Prepare to change your workspace into a more effective and productive one.

Making A Successful Timetable

A crucial aspect of time management is making an efficient timetable. It entails determining priorities, allocating time for critical tasks, and developing a time management strategy. The following actions will assist you in making an efficient schedule:

1. Determine your top priorities: Determine your top priorities for both tasks and goals. These are the most important tasks that must be completed and take up the most time.

2. Compute how long it will take: Calculate the approximate time needed to finish each task. Estimate each task's completion time realistically and provide additional time for unforeseen issues or delays.

3. Create a schedule: Determine when you will work on each activity using a planner or scheduling software. Schedule relaxation

periods, breaks, and time for significant family and personal activities.

4. Employ time blocking: This strategy involves setting aside certain time slots for particular tasks. Doing this ensures you have enough time to do each activity and maintain your attention.

5. Be adaptable: Keep in mind that unforeseen events could occur. Thus, it's critical to be adaptable to your schedule. Should the need arise, be ready to modify your schedule, and don't forget to notify anybody who might be impacted.

6. Regularly review and modify your schedule: Make necessary adjustments by reviewing it regularly. This can help you stay on course and use your time wisely. For instance, you might estimate that it will take you ten hours to finish a high-priority assignment like writing a report for work. Next, you can make a timetable that allows a certain amount of time for this activity;

for example, you could work on it for two hours every day for five days.

To sum up, efficient scheduling is necessary for efficient time management. You may maximise your time and accomplish your objectives by determining your priorities, projecting the time required, creating a timetable, employing time blocking, being adaptable, and routinely evaluating and modifying your calendar.

Methods for Scheduling Time

A common time management strategy is time blocking, setting aside certain time slots for particular tasks. The following are some methods for blocking off time:

1. The Pomodoro Method: Using the Pomodoro Technique, you should divide your work into 25-minute intervals, or "pomodoros," and take brief pauses in between. After completing four Pomodoros, you take a longer break. By employing this strategy, you can keep your focus and avoid burnout. For instance, you may

arrange to answer emails for four Pomodoros in the morning, followed by a lengthier rest. Then, you may plan four Pomodoros for afternoon project work, with a longer break in between.

2. Time Blocking by Activity Category: This method entails allocating time blocks for each activity category and combining related tasks into groups. One such approach could be to allocate a specific time slot for responding to emails, another for making calls, and still another for working on projects. For instance, you may set up 9:00–10:00 am for email checking and replying, 10:00–11:00 am for phone calls, and 11:00–12:00 pm for project work.

3. Time Blocking by Priority: This method entails allocating time slots for high-priority tasks first, followed by lower-priority tasks. This might assist you in concentrating on and completing the most crucial activities. For

instance, you may schedule a time to focus on a high-priority project from 9:00 to 11:00 am, then respond to emails for a while, and finally work on lower-priority activities.

4. Time Blocking by Energy Level: Using this strategy, you may plan high-energy and focused work for when you're most awake and focused throughout the day. Less taxing chores can be planned when you're feeling low on energy. For instance, you may plan to work on energy and concentration from 8:00 to 10:00 am, followed by a break. Then, you may set aside 11:00 am–12:00 pm for lower-energy administrative activities.

5. Time Blocking by Personal Rhythms: This method entails planning time slots per your routines and habits. For instance, if you are an early riser, you should plan to do your most critical work first thing in the morning while you are most focused and awake. For instance, you may plan to work on a project from 8:00 to

10:00 am, then take a break. Next, you may plan to work out or engage in a self-care activity from 10:30 to 11:30 am to help you decompress.

To sum up, time blocking is a flexible approach to time management that you may tailor to your tastes and working style. You may stay focused, be productive, and accomplish your goals by employing strategies like the Pomodoro Technique, time blocking by activity type, priority, energy level, and personal rhythms.

Creating Effective Work Practices

Creating productive work habits is crucial to time management success. Here are some crucial behaviours to think about:

1. Pay attention to one activity at a time: Although multitasking may be tempting, doing so can reduce productivity and raise stress levels. Give each task your whole attention and concentrate until it is finished.

2. Reduce outside distractions: Determine which distractions keep you from being productive and focused, then eliminate them. This may be shutting tabs or windows that aren't needed, turning off notifications on your computer or phone, or finding a quiet workplace.

It can help you maintain focus and refuel. Schedule regular breaks and use the opportunity to stretch, stroll, or engage in other enjoyable activities.

4. Establish deadlines: By establishing deadlines, you can prevent procrastination and keep on task. Establish reasonable and attainable deadlines, and hold yourself responsible for fulfilling them.

5. Learn to delegate: If you're overburdened with work, figure out how to assign part of it to others. This can help you focus on things that

need your attention and expertise and free up time.

6. Maintaining an orderly workspace will help reduce distractions and maintain focus. Spend a few minutes every day keeping your desk clutter-free and organised.

7. Effective time management techniques: Time management techniques are necessary for effective work habits. To maximise your time, set objectives, rank your to-do list, and plan your day.

By forming these effective work habits, you can increase productivity, lessen stress, and accomplish your goals. Recall that it takes time and practice to form new habits, so have patience and remain dedicated to changing for the better.

Additional Devices and Attachments

When setting up your home office, the things on the above list are the most crucial. On the other hand, you can purchase additional accessories to facilitate your work-from-home lifestyle. For calls and meetings, for instance, having a headset is essential. These days, you may also acquire ones that filter out background sounds from your environment. As a result, while you speak, others won't be able to hear your neighbour's dogs barking.

If you buy a larger screen, having a keyboard, mouse, or touchpad is also a good idea. Using these external devices is simpler than using your laptop's keyboard and touchpad. Of course, this won't be required if you use a desktop computer. Also, having a multipurpose printer can be useful, even though we operate mostly in digital format. There are instances when printing or scanning documents is unavoidable.

An uninterruptible power supply (UPS) or surge protector is a great investment for people who work from home. In the event of a power outage, this shields your computer from surges.

Additionally, you can get a tiny UPS for your modem, which will maintain internet access during a blackout. The amount of time your laptop battery will survive before needing to be charged, though, limits this. Even so, it's a terrific alternative because it lets you keep your job and let others know that you won't be available immediately rather than being disconnected immediately.

You can also have speakers if you enjoy listening to music while working. This will enhance audio quality and eliminate the need for constant headphone use. For a workspace, a smart assistant is also not a bad idea. Not only will it store your thoughts for later, but it will also aid in your memory of crucial calls and meetings. When working, I frequently get an idea or thought and ask my smart assistant to record it for later. If hiring an office assistant is out of the question, a whiteboard can work just as well. It will help you work on things visually or quickly scribble down items to remember later. If you utilise it to organise your day, it can also assist you in being more productive.

A yoga mat is another fantastic item to have on a desk. Working from home makes it simple to become engrossed for hours and forget to take little breaks. This is why treadmills and standing desks have been so well-liked lately. However, having a yoga mat close by will serve as a helpful reminder to take a few minutes to pause and exercise your body. Your body will appreciate the impact of even a few easy stretches. Plants on your desk are also a terrific way to improve your mood. Having plants around will also motivate you to check on their growth or water them sometimes.

Give up trying to be flawless.

The pursuit of perfection can be emotionally and mentally draining. Therefore, single mothers must let go of it. Being a single parent frequently entails many duties and difficulties, and attempting to uphold an unattainable standard of perfection simply causes needless strain and worry.

When they accept their shortcomings, single mothers may concentrate on what matters—giving their kids love, support, and a loving environment. It also promotes self-compassion by letting them realise that, despite the demands of their work, they are trying their best.

Furthermore, recognising flaws can teach kids resilience and the value of accepting themselves—two important life lessons. Essentially, realising that it's acceptable to be flawed gives single mothers the confidence to put their happiness and their kids' happiness above impossible expectations, which eventually results in a more contented and balanced family life.

Seek motivation to support your path as a single mother.

Being a single parent can be challenging and complex, leaving many wondering how to be a successful single mother.

It's important to remember that you are not the only one going through these difficulties. There are many positive examples of accomplished single parents who have raised outstanding kids and made outstanding accomplishments.

Take the legacies of former Presidents Obama and Clinton, raised by single parents, as an example. Their experiences remind you that you are not alone in facing and overcoming comparable challenges.

You can also get ideas from the people in your social circle. Maybe you have a buddy who has succeeded as a single parent and can be a reliable confidant with insightful counsel and support. Connecting with these people can provide you with support and a feeling of community while you deal with the difficulties of being a single parent.

It's important to maintain your resolve and not give up on single parenthood—especially on those difficult days when it seems too much to bear.

Even if the road could be difficult, it's also a fantastic chance to raise and develop a remarkable human being.

Accept the encouragement of your loved ones and the examples of successful single parents as sources of motivation to help you along this amazing and fulfilling journey.

Recall that you are not just enduring your role as a single mother but thriving in it.

How To Put The Pomodoro Technique Into Practice

1980s as a time management method based on the notion that working in uninterrupted blocks is productive.

You will need a timer to apply the Pomodoro technique. While the term "pomodoro" refers to the sort of kitchen tomato that Cirillo used at his institution, you are not required to use one of them. You can use any timer these days—many digital programs are even available for this purpose.

To begin utilising the method, take the following actions:

1. Choosing a task: Decide what you wish to work on; this can be study or work. The size of this task should be just right—it should demand focus without being overly demanding.

2. Timing: Assign twenty-five minutes. The idea behind these "pomodoros" is to spend this time

working on your homework without interruption.

3. begin working on your homework: Get started on your homework. If an idea or side work distracts you, jot it down for later and return your attention to your primary task.

4. End of the tomato: Take a moment to record on paper that you have finished a Pomodoro when the timer goes off. You'll feel a sense of achievement when you cross off each finished Pomodoro.

5. brief rest: Take a five-minute break following each Pomodoro. During this pause, your brain absorbs information better and gets ready for the next Pomodoro.

6. extended rest: It is advised to take a longer break, between 15 and 30 minutes, following the completion of four Pomodoros. This extended period of rest aids in recharging your mind for the upcoming work periods.

You must honour the customs of the day. Use the extra time if you complete a task before the Pomodoro is up to evaluate your work or get ready for the next one. Don't worry if you can't complete the assignment in time. Simply carry on with it throughout the following Pomodoro.

In addition to helping you become more productive, the Pomodoro approach teaches you to work with time rather than against it. As long as you stick to its core principles of focused labour interspersed with rest intervals, this strategy is adaptable and can be tailored to your unique requirements.

Examples of the Pomodoro technique in practice

1980s as a time management method to increase output and improve the calibre of work. We'll now go on to some real-world examples that show how this method might be used in everyday situations.

Example 1: Examine

Let's say you need to prepare for a significant test. You break up your reading material into manageable chunks, each taking about twenty-five minutes to finish. You set a timer for twenty-five minutes (called, traditionally, a "pomodoro," which is Italian for "tomato," and utilised by Francesco Cirillo in his kitchens) and go to work studying. You focus entirely on your work during this period and keep yourself from being distracted. After the five minutes are up, you take a rest. After completing four repetitions of this "Pomodoro" cycle, you should take a lengthier break, lasting between 15 and 30 minutes. By the end of the day, you'll have developed regular breaks that help avoid exhaustion and have studied more efficiently.

Example 2: Tasks and Assignments

You have to perform various activities, such as testing software, writing code, and resolving bugs. These chores can be divided into 25-minute blocks using the Pomodoro technique, which enables you to concentrate on one activity at a time and then take a quick break before moving on to the next. By doing this, you can keep up a steady work rate and prevent the overwhelm of taking on a project this size.

Example #3: Cleaning

When taken as a whole, household tasks like laundry and housecleaning can appear overwhelming. Nevertheless, applying the Pomodoro approach can divide these chores into more doable chunks. For instance, you could clean the bathroom for a "pomodoro," take a five-minute break, and then go to the kitchen. Using this method can help you avoid procrastinating and make chores appear less tiresome.

Chapter Two

Taking Command of Your Life: Techniques for Achieving Your Objectives

Taking Charge of Your Life is the process of controlling one's behaviour and decision-making to accomplish a desired result or objective. It is also referred to as self-governance or self-discipline. It is essential to success and personal growth because it empowers people's goals and values.

Taking initiative rather than reacting is one of the main advantages of self-rule. Individuals are at the mercy of other individuals or external causes when they depend on others to direct their behaviour. Nonetheless, people can actively mould their lives and produce the desired results when they accept accountability for their choices and actions.

Self-rule also fosters reflection and self-awareness, which is a positive. People in charge of their behaviour are more inclined to think back on what they do and how it affects others and themselves. Making more deliberate and thoughtful decisions might result from having a deeper awareness of oneself and one's motivations.

People who rely on themselves rather than others to direct their actions are more autonomous and independent. This might result from increased self-worth and confidence, as well as a feeling of empowerment and agency.

Self-control, however, can often be difficult since it calls on people to accept accountability for their deeds and make tough decisions. Maintaining self-control and consistency in one's behaviour can also be challenging, particularly when faced with distractions or temptations.

People can practise goal-setting and achievement, form healthy habits, and increase their self-awareness and self-knowledge to create self-rule. It's crucial to have patience with oneself and to have reasonable expectations for oneself.

Surrounding oneself with helpful people and circumstances can also help one become more self-reliant. This can involve asking those who have succeeded in the areas one wants to improve for mentoring or advice. It may also entail setting up a physical space that encourages productivity and self-control.

To sum up, self-control is crucial to success and personal growth. It enables people to take charge of their lives, make decisions according to their goals and values, and bring about the results they are hoping for. But it also calls for perseverance, consistency, and discipline. Individuals can acquire the abilities and mindset required to successfully control themselves and accomplish their goals with practice and assistance.

Ways to use self-rule to accomplish objectives

Establishing definite and precise goals: It's critical to know exactly what you want to accomplish and ensure your goals are time-bound, relevant, measurable, and explicit. This makes progress more concrete and attainable while also serving to give direction and concentration.

Specifying Objectives and Approaches

To succeed in any aspect of life, it is necessary to establish well-defined objectives. Setting and completing clear, specific goals advance in a particular area, advance professionally, or simply progress in your chosen field. From a self-rule standpoint, this article will discuss the significance of establishing precise goals and offer advice and techniques for creating and accomplishing your objectives.

Setting precise and unambiguous goals is crucial because it gives one a distinct purpose and direction. Achieving your objective when you are clear about what you want to accomplish. This might support you in maintaining your motivation and direction in the face of difficulties or setbacks.

Setting precise, well-defined goals also has the benefit of enabling you to track your advancement. When you have a specific objective in mind, this has the potential to be inspiring and maintain your focus on your objective.

Finding out what you want to accomplish is a necessary first step to developing clear and precise goals. Setting relevant objectives that align with your priorities and values may require some thought and time. After determining your objectives, dividing them into smaller, more doable targets is critical. It will be simpler to monitor your development and maintain motivation.

Setting a deadline for yourself is a crucial tactic for accomplishing your objectives. And maintaining motivation and focus. It's crucial to ensure that your objectives are both ambitious and doable. Demotivating goals are too difficult to achieve, while too-easy goals will not inspire as much.

Ensuring that goals are specific is a crucial component of goal-setting. This implies that you must be able to gauge your development and recognise when you've reached your objective. Setting and sticking to specific goals also facilitates the creation of an action plan.

I can still clearly recall the moment I realised my life was meaningless. I counted the minutes until I could leave work while sitting at my desk. I didn't feel motivated or fulfilled. I knew I needed to change but was unsure where to begin.

That's when I decided to give myself clear goals. I knew that having goals would help me keep motivated and focused by giving me something to strive for.

Initially, I considered my long-term goals and objectives. I decided to raise my salary by 20% over the following year because I understood I wanted to be financially secure. I also set a goal to lose 20 pounds in the next six months to be in better shape.

I then divided these objectives into more achievable, smaller steps. For instance, I planned to go to industry events, network more, and take on more work responsibilities to boost my salary. I set out to eat a healthier diet, exercise frequently, and monitor my progress to reduce weight.

I discovered that I had greater energy and motivation than ever before when I started to work towards my objectives. Every morning, I looked forward to waking up and starting my day. I was also pleased with myself for moving forward and accomplishing my objectives.

A significant obstacle I encountered was maintaining my motivation when times were hard. I discovered it was simple to lose motivation when I encountered obstacles or didn't immediately see results. However, I had to remind myself that improvement takes time and that it's crucial to acknowledge little victories along the road.

Finding a way to balance my aspirations with other responsibilities in my life was another difficulty. I came to understand the value of flexibility and realism and the necessity of preventing my aspirations from taking over my life.

A year later, I can confidently state that my life has improved due to setting clear goals. In addition to losing twenty-five pounds and increasing my income by twenty-five per cent, I now feel I have a purpose. I've also realised that goal-making is an ongoing process. Thus, I will keep creating and achieving new objectives in the future.

I strongly advise everyone who feels uninspired or unfulfilled to set precise goals. Although it could be challenging initially, the benefits will ultimately be worthwhile. You'll not only accomplish your goals, but you'll also experience a valuable sense of fulfilment and success.

Techniques for Setting Priorities

Assume Ariel has five objectives. She knows they adhere strictly to SMART, but there's another issue. She doesn't know where to begin. Luckily for us, the answer to prioritisation is simple. We'll utilise Ariel for our next instances; she has a frequent issue. Many of the "time traps" Alec Mackenzie discusses in his book can be caused by a lack of priorities. I found that a good quarter of the traps had a cause similar to a lack of priorities by quickly reading the useful description of each trap's causes and solutions at the end of the book.

Thus establishing Ariel even more. She attends her community college and is majoring in communications. She accepts a summer internship and soon discovers that her schedule is disrupted, as though she is no longer in charge. Her ambitions seem silly and unachievable, and her priorities are everywhere. Ariel only needs a few more moves to reclaim the initiative. As her supervisor makes clear, she needs to learn how to prioritise the chores throughout the day. He suggests that she study the Eisenhower Matrix, the same technique we will use.

We'll first study the Eisenhower Matrix to mitigate this. Though it has an intimidating moniker, the strategy is rather straightforward, according to studies conducted by Bratterudet. Imagine a square and divide it into four sectors, according to al (2020). The two upper-half sectors are set aside for critical work. Conversely, the bottom two are for insignificant stuff. We'll divide the left and right sides similarly. The tasks we consider urgent will be on our left, and the duties we consider not urgent will be on our right. We will now divide our square into four distinct quadrants, which are as follows:

The "Do" quadrant is set aside for pressing and significant tasks. Put another way, the things most important to your life or profession should come first.

"Schedule" Quadrant: This one is in the upper-right quadrant and contains significant tasks that can wait until the next day or two. Calendar-friendly tasks are perfect for this, like calling a loved one or going to a symposium on a subject you're passionate about.

"Delegate" Quadrant: Urgent yet unimportant duties are in our bottom-left section. These frequently don't match your values or skill set as well. They still need to be dealt with promptly and effectively, though. To help them, you may either recommend someone more qualified for the job or empower the individual for whom this would be in the upper right hand by providing them with resources or knowledge.

"Disregard" Quadrant: Items that are neither urgent nor significant are in the bottom right corner. Procrastinating tendencies are frequently included in this category. And you should just refrain from engaging in them, as simple as it may sound.

Using Ariel as an example, she can decide what to do with each activity in her day based on her goals. Three are marked as important and urgent by her, while seven are significant but not urgent. Throughout the day, she also had to handle a few minor but necessary duties, which she could assign to available coworkers. Even though none of her objectives fell into the latter category, she still had to resist browsing social media's short-form content. Overall, she could make her day clearer using the Eisenhower Matrix. For a start, not bad!

Our collection of effective tools also includes the Pareto Principle. It helps us distinguish between tasks that must be completed immediately and those that can wait, just like the Eisenhower Matrix did. In a 2018 medical article, the authors leveraged their knowledge and concluded that a Pareto chart would identify the areas that need attention. The article states, "[it] holds that a small number of factors have a disproportionate impact on any outcome." And just as they had anticipated, 78% of the issues in their workflow were caused by a single reason.

As a general rule, one can approach the Pareto Principle. In other words, 20% of the cause of a particular event yields 80% of the result. This also holds for time management: 80% of a task can be completed with the right 20% of our effort. Unfortunately, the opposite is also true, and the final 20% of polish will contain 80% of our labour.

Prioritisation is where this theory is useful, though. You're good at some things, which applies to work and play. Determine high-impact jobs and concentrate on them using your field knowledge, particularly in urgent projects. As you resolve a greater number of issues, you'll see that this greatly increases the efficiency of your work.

In both cases, what should be done with significant but non-urgent work is unclear. Strangely, most seasoned practitioners weigh the most assignments in their Scheduling quadrant. Crises can help explain part of this, as they frequently involve unexpectedly urgent duties. However, it also fits with the Eisenhower Matrix's initial concept. Stated the acknowledged inventor and former president.

The Merger And Acquisition Of

Action plan: Determine which tasks you can assign or outsource to save time for more important endeavours.

In the fast-paced world of today, time is a precious commodity. Whether you are an individual seeking a better work-life balance or a professional, your secret weapon may be the ability to delegate and outsource. You may reclaim hours from your day by using this action plan to discover tasks that can be assigned or outsourced. After reading this comprehensive guide, you'll have the knowledge and assurance to improve productivity, simplify your processes, and focus on what matters.

Authority Delegation

Delegation is a strategic technique that helps you be a better leader and decision-maker than just allocating tasks. Learn the art of delegation, from setting clear objectives to choosing the most qualified team members. Learn how delegating can help you be more productive.

Selecting Tasks That Can Be Delegated

Not every task is made equal. Determine which duties can be assigned to others. We'll talk about the prerequisites for delegation, such as tasks that are repetitive, time-consuming, or beyond your area of competence. Look for hidden gems that will allow you more time on your hands.

The Advantages of Contracting Out

Outsourcing advances delegation by adding outside knowledge. Discover more about outsourcing, from freelancers to specialized businesses. Understand how outsourcing can provide efficient solutions at a reasonable cost while optimizing results.

Creating Your Outsourcing and Delegation Strategy

Make a special action plan that satisfies your goals and the resources available. To ensure success, we'll go into detail about developing a delegation strategy, selecting an outsourced budget, and determining critical performance indicators.

How to Control the Process of Delegation

It could be challenging to delegate without clear guidance. Discover the logical steps of effective delegation, including task selection, communication, progress monitoring, and offering constructive feedback.

The Fundamentals of Contracting

With confidence, start your outsourcing journey. Under the title of Outsourcing Basics, this chapter covers finding trustworthy partners, negotiating contracts, protecting intellectual property, and forming long-term collaborations.

Overcoming Challenges in Delegation

Delegation presents challenges. Learn how to overcome common challenges such as trust issues, a fear of losing control, and communication blunders.

Evaluation of Achievement and Continuous Improvement

Record your attempts at delegating and outsourcing. Acknowledge the use of feedback loops and KPIs in achievement measurement. Learn the concepts of continuous improvement to gradually improve your strategies.

True Case Studies

Find real-world case studies of individuals and businesses that have successfully delegated and outsourced. Find out how these strategies altered their business practices and increased production.

Using Your Plan

Apply the knowledge you have just gained right now. Create a detailed action plan that considers your goals, available resources, and challenges. Take the first steps towards living a more productive, balanced life.

Delegation and outsourcing are life skills that can help you redefine your priorities and increase productivity. Equipped with the information and tools in this book, you can take control of your schedule and do more than you ever thought possible. It's time to assign and outsource to maximize your potential.

Establish guidelines to help you manage the conduct of others.

Establish your definition of client crises and the situations in which you will intervene.

kin

With family members, you can follow the same procedure. If your partner usually communicates during your OUT, discuss emergencies and schedule regular conversation times.

A partner will frequently feel more important because of this since they will know you are making time for them specifically.

Instruments

People cause the majority of interruptions from devices. The good news is that we have command over these gadgets. All of them can be momentarily turned off.

Procedures

Choose the process-oriented interruptions from your list. Make two categories now: avoidable and unpreventable.

It is possible to stop a lot of process interruptions. Computer viruses, low inventory, running out of supplies, etc. The majority of these kinds of disruption ought to be eliminated with a little forethought and the implementation of fresh strategies.

Certain process disruptions cannot be avoided. Equipment failures, cash flow issues, power outages, etc.

Certain unavoidable business disruptions can be "cured."

- Backup generators can prevent power disruptions.
- Having a cash reserve for equipment replacement, backing up computers, having backup equipment, or having solid technical support contacts on staff or retainer can all assist in preventing equipment malfunctions.
- Establishing a line of credit, cash reserves, or credit cards can help alleviate cash flow problems.

Monitoring Disruptions

Individuals Handle Lost Device Time Interruptions

Sums

Add up all of your time and record any interruptions.

5.

4

3.

Persons Two Devices One Process

0

Weeks One, Two, Three, and Four

Once you've tracked them for four weeks, you'll have a decent notion of where your interruptions are coming from.

Though you can't always halt interruptions or influence other people's actions, as this chapter's title suggests, you can 'Minimise' disruptions to have greater control over your time.

Finding Time Thieves and Apprehending Them

How much of the time you spend at work is truly productive? Most of us spend innumerable hours doing things repeatedly, responding to circumstances that never should have happened, and complaining about how much work we have to get done in the limited amount of time we have. We must become conscious of our behaviours to determine where we spend all of our time.

Record your work activities in a journal for at least one week. Although this might be very time-consuming and seem to take up even more of your valuable time, we must learn to be conscious of how we spend our time if we want to improve our time management. You often use "time as if you had more and more forever," as the Roman philosopher Seneca once observed.

Examine your log once you've finished it. Keep an eye out for time wasters. Anything that lessens your productivity at work is a time stealer. Examples include taking on tasks that you ought to have assigned to others, taking excessively long to respond to or send emails, and making pointless phone calls.

Talks, staff interruptions, drawn-out meetings, rushing through tasks that ought to have been finished sooner, attempting to do too much at once, redoing someone else's work because it is subpar, completing tasks more than once, lacking knowledge or skills, poor planning, sleep deprivation, difficulty saying "no," and lacking a daily schedule in place.

How is the time passing you by?

Many small and medium-sized business owners are so preoccupied with managing their companies daily that they fail to notice the passing of time. Before they know it, it's 6:00 p.m., and they probably won't be able to tell you what they've accomplished.

Making a journal of your activities and their times will help you track where your time is going and solve time management issues.

Concluding

We've covered the importance of leadership in time management in this chapter and how to set a positive example for your team and foster productivity. You can establish a productive workplace and more quickly accomplish your business objectives by setting an example of effective time management, setting clear expectations, offering assistance and training, acknowledging and rewarding achievement, promoting a culture of productivity, and supporting work-life balance. Remember that sustained work and attention are necessary for effective leadership, so periodically evaluate your progress and make necessary adjustments.

Practice: Carry Out a Time Audit

Doing a time audit is one method to enhance your leadership abilities in time management. You may optimize your schedule by using this exercise to determine how you presently spend your time and where you can make changes.

Guidelines:

1. Use a pen and paper or a time tracking tool to record your time during a weeklong period, preferably during a weekday.

2. Sort your activities into many categories, like emails, meetings, working on projects, interacting with people, and administrative duties.

3. Examine the information to find areas where you can best utilize your time. For example, you might discover that you're spending too much time on administrative duties that might be assigned to someone else or at meetings that could be shortened or removed.

4. Create a strategy for modifying your timetable to maximize your efficiency. This could be assigning responsibilities to others, shortening the duration of meetings, or setting up particular hours for unbroken work.

5. Follow through on your plan and monitor your progress. To improve your schedule and boost productivity, keep a close eye on how much time you spend using it and adapt as necessary.

You may set an excellent example for your team and show them how to manage their time effectively by performing a time audit and making necessary adjustments to your calendar.

4-Awareness of Operations Management Techniques for Optimising Efficiencies and Simplifying Procedures.

Understanding and streamlining your company's processes as an owner is essential to its success. In this chapter, We'll review the fundamentals of operations management, process simplification techniques, and efficiency maximization.

1. Operations management: what is it?

The process of planning, executing, and refining company processes to maximize productivity and effectiveness is known as operations management. Accomplishing company objectives entails managing people, procedures, and resources.

2. Determine Crucial Business Procedures

Finding your essential business procedures is the first step towards streamlining operations. This could involve Everything from marketing and customer service to production and manufacturing. After determining which business procedures are essential, you can begin evaluating their effectiveness and pinpointing areas for development.

3. Assess Performance Indicators

Finding areas where your business processes can be optimized requires measuring performance measures. This could entail monitoring supply chain performance, evaluating consumer comments, or measuring production levels. By monitoring these indicators, you can find areas for improvement, inefficiencies, and bottlenecks.

4. Create Standard Operating Procedures.

SOPs, or standard operating procedures, are crucial for reducing processes and guaranteeing uniformity throughout your company. SOPs minimize waste and increase the likelihood of error-free task performance by giving precise instructions on how to do activities.

5. Automate Procedures

cut down on mistakes, and free up team members for more crucial work. Software for inventory management, order processing automation, and customer support inquiry processing are a few examples.

Chapter 11: Managers' Guide To Effective Time Management

Finding a successful manager who lacks time management and staffing skills is like searching for a unicorn. You won't because they don't exist. Everyone has the same hours in a day to do the things that need to be done, and how you spend your time determines how effective you are at achieving those things.

Whether you're a first-time manager or simply need a refresher course, knowing and applying effective time management skills will help you thrive in your career.

Before we go into effective time management strategies for managers, let's first discuss the "why" and "what" of time management. Time management is a straightforward strategy for organizing how to use a day's 24 hours to accomplish personal and professional tasks.

The Eisenhower Matrix, developed by US President Dwight Eisenhower, separated time management into four categories:

Do it first, then make a plan, allocate tasks, and stop doing it.

Each skill associated with time management has a place in this matrix. If you can learn to split your tasks and time into digestible portions without going crazy, you can lead your team and accomplish goals.

1. possess a thorough understanding of goal-setting

As said by Benjamin Franklin,

If you are not making a plan, you are intending to fail.

The Founding Fathers got it right, and knowing how to set goals for your group is important. Establishing goals is crucial, so make sure they can be divided into tasks that are done.

For example, if your company aims to boost website traffic by 10% over a year, you should define quantifiable goals every week, month, and six months to ensure the goal stays on track.

Take a look at these articles for tips on creating short- and long-term goals:

2. Good Communication Can Transform Everything

Effective communication has the power to build or destroy any kind of relationship, personal or professional, and it often breaks down when a manager struggles with time management. However, the ability of a manager to communicate effectively with their staff and clients while also listening can have a big impact on the success of the business.

You can ensure that your team members work towards well-defined goals by maintaining regular contact with them. A manager engaging in frequent and open client interaction has a better chance of witnessing their business grow. Use your time wisely by speaking with thoughtfulness.

3. The Value of Structure

For managers to effectively manage their time, assigned jobs and actual labour must be well-organized. If your team lacks organization and members don't know their roles or where to seek help, all your goals will be unsuccessful.

Being well-organized and communicating well is essential for maximizing one's time.

Regarding how you keep your workspace organized, well, that's up to you. If you like to have a disorganized bedroom at home, that's OK, but disarray has no place in business. You could have been more productive with every minute looking for a misplaced file.

4. The Value of Skillful Delegation

If you delegate well, your team members will be more equipped to work with assurance and efficiency. As a manager, it is your responsibility to assign the tasks that correspond with each job to the members of your team who are most qualified for them. You and your team will waste time if you don't set up work.

If you properly assign different duties to your team members and ensure they have Everything they need to complete them, they will be less dependent on you to complete the job.

5. Arrange Appropriate Tasks for Appropriate Times

If you were building a car, you wouldn't try to install the sound system before the frame was in place, would you?

The first block of the Eisenhower Matrix, Do First, tells you to decide which tasks are most crucial to finish before moving on to the next one. It may be something small, like answering a question from your supervisor, or something larger, like completing the specifics of a brand-new social media plan.

The secret is understanding how to prioritize your tasks daily based on their urgency, completion time, and recommended time.

6. Recognize the Dangers of Multitasking

Everybody has a lot of work, but some things will inevitably fall to the ground if we try to do it all at once. It's way too easy to get into work and then, when your phone beeps, stop to check your email. This causes your brain to work harder to catch up, which is a horrible way to lose attention.

Instead, set aside designated times during the day to read and reply to emails. If you focus on one thing at a time, you'll finish the work more quickly and with full attention.

Time-Management Strategies

It takes planning, focus, and discipline to manage time well. This chapter will examine various time management strategies to help us maximise our time, boost output, and accomplish our objectives.

The Pomodoro Technique: This method divides your workday into 25-minute halves and requires a 5-minute rest. You take a lengthier pause of 20 to 30 minutes after four intervals. You may prevent burnout and maintain focus by using this strategy, which divides your job into small, achievable tasks.

Using the Eisenhower Matrix, jobs are divided into four groups according to their urgency and significance. These fall into four categories: not important or urgent, not urgent but important, not urgent but important, and urgent but not important. Have the biggest influence on your objectives by ranking them according to significance and urgency.

Time blocking: This method entails setting aside time in blocks for designated jobs or endeavours. This aids in preventing distractions and maintaining your attention on one work at a time. It also guarantees that you allocate adequate time to significant assignments and undertakings.

The Ivy Lee Method: This method entails setting a daily priority list of six things to be completed and concentrating on finishing them before tackling other tasks. This keeps you focused on what matters most and prevents you from getting overwhelmed by a lengthy to-do list.

States that 20% of your efforts should yield 80% of your results. You may boost your productivity and do more work in less time by concentrating on the projects with the biggest impact.

Single-tasking: This method entails concentrating on a single task simultaneously, blocking out distractions. This can be especially useful for assignments that call for a high level of concentration and focus.

Timeboxing: This method gives a task or project a set amount of time and concentrates on doing it within the allotted period. This can be helpful for jobs that tend to become larger to fit the available time.

These methods are only a handful of the numerous time management strategies. It's crucial to try various methods to determine which suits you the most. Recall that time is money and that each minute lost is one that we cannot get back. By employing efficient time management strategies, we may maximise our time, boost output, and accomplish our objectives.

Review and Make New Objectives

A change could have an impact on your long-term goals and aspirations. Give your objectives a second look and adjust them to reflect the current situation. This approach has the potential to be empowering, rekindling your enthusiasm and drive to reach even bigger goals.

For instance, a software development business discovered fresh prospects in the developing domain of artificial intelligence. They increased the scope of their product offerings and obtained a competitive advantage by establishing new objectives in line with this technology.

Effective Communication

Navigating change requires effective communication. Maintain communication with your team, particularly if you're working remotely. Use technology, such as email, Slack, or video calls, to keep everyone informed and involved. These can help you build solid relationships.

Think about a marketing company that made the switch to remote work. They created a feeling of community, promoted open communication, and preserved a strong team culture by utilising virtual communication tools. They were able to adjust to change and become more creative and productive due to this technique.

Gain Resilience

Although adapting to change can be difficult, doing so will help you stay composed and on task. Here are some methods for honing this essential ability:

Recognise that life and business are full of change.

To assist in the processing of emotions, express your thoughts and feelings.

Determine which areas of change you have influence over and which you do not. When unsure, pay attention to what you can control and ask for help or guidance.

Accepting change necessitates resilience, an optimistic outlook, good communication, and goal reevaluation. By implementing these tactics, you and your group can find chances for development and achievement in addition to adjusting to new problems.

Acquiring Knowledge From Errors

Acknowledging that making errors is an inherent aspect of being human is critical. Mistakes or setbacks will occur periodically for you and your staff as remote work becomes more popular. Nonetheless, these occurrences can provide insightful teaching moments that enhance decision-making and professional partnerships.

To effectively learn from your mistakes, take the following actions:

Step 1: Own Up to Your Mistakes

Show sincere regret and accept accountability for your mistakes. By being open and honest with your coworkers, you can establish confidence in your professional relationships by demonstrating that the error was accidental.

Step 2: Recognise the Primary Cause

Determine what went wrong, why it happened, and how to keep it from happening again. For instance, if you didn't send a crucial report because it wasn't scheduled, ensure you are better prepared by carefully tracking your assignments and due dates.

Step 3: Request Input

Speak with supervisors and coworkers to get their advice and avoid past mistakes. Positive feedback can help people advance both personally and professionally.

Step 4: Look for the bright side

Every negative experience presents a chance for growth. Realising where you are, you may make a bad circumstance a worthwhile learning experience.

Step5: Use the Knowledge Acquired

Put the techniques and answers you've found into practice to stop making the same mistakes. Make sure you apply these skills to your everyday routine to achieve sustained progress.

Step 6: Give Your Knowledge Away

Share your knowledge with your coworkers to foster a culture of growth and learning. Through a collaborative discussion of typical mistakes, your team may effectively prevent and resolve them.

Step 7: Engage in Self-Examination

Examine your activities, achievements, and lessons learnt regularly. This self-examination approach helps you identify your progress and emphasises the value of taking lessons from your experiences.

How to Pick the Finest Tricks and Advice for Your Type,

These hints and techniques don't apply to every situation. Depending on the individual's personality, interests, or circumstances, they could function differently for each person. As a result, you must choose the finest tricks and advice for yourself using some standards, such as:

● The type of person you are: Your preferred method of processing information, making decisions, arranging your workload, or interacting with others could be different. For instance, if you're an introvert, you might prefer to work alone in a quiet, private setting with no distractions or interruptions. Being an extrovert, you could enjoy working in or stimulation. To learn more about your strengths and weaknesses and determine your personality type, you can take personality tests like the Enneagram, the Big Five Personality

Traits (OCEAN), and the Myers-Briggs Type Indicator (MBTI).

● Your learning style: You might choose to learn new concepts, abilities, or knowledge differently. For instance, if you are a visual learner, you might prefer to study by watching films, diagrams, or photographs. If you're an auditory learner, you could enjoy listening to podcasts, music, or lectures. Playing games, doing experiments, or engaging in hands-on activities may be more appealing to kinesthetic learners. You can take learning style assessments like the VARK model, Kolb's Learning Style Inventory, or Honey and Mumford Learning Style Questionnaire to learn more about your learning preferences and strengths and weaknesses.

● Your circumstances: An entirely different circumstance may impact your time management and productivity. For instance, if you're a student, you might have to juggle your coursework with extracurricular activities, a part-time job, or your social life. If you are a parent, you might have to juggle employment in addition to childcare duties, household chores, and obligations to your family. As a freelancer, you might have to balance your clients' demands, deadlines, and payments and your tasks. You must consider your circumstances while selecting the tricks and advice that best fit your objectives.

You can boost your chances of effectively implementing the greatest advice and shortcuts and advance your productivity and time management abilities by selecting the best ones for yourself.

Establishing A Habit Of Time Management

How to develop habits out of time management techniques

Productive performance is a prerequisite for successful time management in both the personal and professional spheres. Time management techniques can be beneficial, but you must make them a regular part of your life to get the most out of them. Why is it vital to go from strategy to habit? Automatic behaviours that we carry out without thinking about them are called habits, and they help us save energy and continue to be productive over time.

At first, it may seem difficult to make time management techniques a habit in our everyday lives. But we can make this shift easier if we take the appropriate measures. We will provide a thorough tutorial on how to accomplish this below.

Determine your time-management techniques: Understanding your time-management techniques inside and out is the first step towards making them a habit. Make a note of every strategy you have, both past and present, and refer to it as you start to form new habits.

Describe your goals: When a strategy has a defined goal, it gets ingrained. Establish your goals for each time management technique. Which would you prefer—more free time, less stress, increased productivity, or all of the above? Setting and achieving a specific goal will keep you motivated as new habits are formed.

Create signals Automatic reactions to cues from our surroundings make up our habits. It may be simpler to develop time management habits if you link your techniques to certain indicators. For instance, if you plan to tackle challenging assignments first thing in the morning, your signal could be your morning cup of coffee.

Maintain consistency: It takes repetition to create a habit. To strengthen this behaviour and eventually make it automatic, apply your time management techniques every day or on the days you have designated.

Rewarded: Reward-induced positive brain responses can strengthen the development of new habits. Give yourself a tiny incentive each time you use a time management technique. A little break, your favourite food, or simply a minute to acknowledge and appreciate your accomplishment could suffice.

Accept setbacks: Developing new habits is a process, and obstacles are common. Don't be hard on yourself if you forget to use a time management technique one day. Rather, accept the loss, comprehend what went wrong and how to avoid it in the future, and move on.

Guarantees other people's support: Encouragement from friends, family, or coworkers can strongly encourage the development of time management techniques into routines. If you tell someone you trust about your objectives and plans, they may be able to provide you with important accountability and support.

As you strive to make your time management techniques a habit, assess your success regularly and make any adjustments. Check to see if these tactics are becoming second nature, and if not, modify your strategy accordingly.

Changing from time management techniques to habits is gradual and calls for perseverance. However, by taking these actions, you can facilitate the development of habits and optimize the advantages of your time management techniques. Remember to take things one step at a time, recognize your successes, and adjust as needed. If you are committed and persistent, you will eventually discover that these tactics come naturally to you, giving you more time to concentrate on other crucial areas of your life.

Chapter 6: Collaboration and Communication Done Right

Engage in active dialogue and focused listening. Good communication is essential to both productive teamwork and efficient time management. Active listening involves understanding and paying attention to what other people are saying. Avoid interrupting others, and try to explain and summarise what you hear to guarantee that everyone understands each other. Communicate clearly and concisely using appropriate channels and materials. Recognize that your body language and tone of voice can influence how others understand your words. Promote straightforward communication and active listening to help dispel myths and foster productive teamwork. Virtual communication with technology

In an increasingly digital and remote workplace, virtual communication is critical. Utilize technological tools and platforms to facilitate communication and teamwork. Hold in-person meetings via video conference whenever feasible to build rapport and a sense of connection. Use project management software and messaging applications to exchange information and keep in constant contact. Set clear guidelines and expectations for online communication to ensure effective and fruitful collaboration. By utilizing technology for virtual collaboration, you may overcome geographical constraints and boost productivity.

Setting expectations and timelines for tasks Setting clear expectations and deadlines is crucial for effective time management and teamwork. Communicating project objectives, deliverables, and deadlines to every team member is important. Ensure that everyone understands their responsibilities. Collaboratively set timelines while taking team members' workloads and availability into account. Provide regular updates on your progress and address any issues or roadblocks that may arise. Establishing guidelines and timelines ensures that tasks are completed on schedule and creates a framework for productive teamwork.

Providing constructive feedback and encouraging a happy work environment. Feedback is essential for both good communication and teamwork. Provide insightful feedback to your team members, focusing on specific actions and outcomes. Give your words a lot of thought and come up with suggestions for improvement. Encourage your workplace to be a place where ideas are valued and accepted. Honour contributions from team members and celebrate successes. Promote open and sincere communication to accommodate a variety of opinions and views. It may promote efficient teamwork and increase overall productivity.

Effective teamwork and communication are essential to time management success. You may expedite information sharing and collaboration by employing technology for virtual communication, active listening strategies, and clear communication. setting guidelines

2.2 Creating SMART Objectives

"specific, measurable, achievable, relevant, and time-bound" are abbreviated as "SMART." It offers a structure for establishing specific, doable, and realistic goals. An explanation of each part is provided below:

1. Specific: Your objective must be precise and well-defined, with no opportunity for interpretation. A clear objective answers the

questions of who, what, where, when, and why. In 3 months, exercising four times a week and maintaining a healthy diet," as opposed to a general one like, "I want to get in shape."

2. Measurable: Your objective should include quantifiable criteria to monitor your progress and establish when the target has been reached. Setting and achieving measurable goals helps you stay motivated because you can monitor your development and acknowledge your successes. Rather than stating "I want to save more money," a measurable objective may be "I want to save $5,000 in 12 months."

3. Achievable: Considering your current abilities, limitations, and resources, your objective should be reasonable and doable. Setting difficult objectives is important, but they shouldn't be unachievable. Unrealistic goals can cause dissatisfaction and demotivation. Make sure your objectives are difficult but doable.

4. Relevant: Your aim should align with your life's purpose, long-term goals, and values. A worthwhile objective that improves your life is relevant. A related goal would be, "I will leave work on time three days a week to spend more time with my family," for instance, if you value work-life balance.

5. Time-bound: Your objective must have an end date or a specified amount of time to be accomplished. In addition to instilling a sense of urgency, deadlines can keep you motivated and focused on completing your task. An example of a time-bound objective is " within one year" instead of "I want to learn Spanish."

You may make sure that your goals are specific, doable, and appropriate for your particular situation by utilizing the SMART criteria while setting them. Consequently, this can assist you in maintaining your motivation, attention, and progress towards your goals.

2.3 Forming an Action Schedule

The next stage after defining your SMART goals is to draft an action plan to guide you towards achieving them. An action plan is a thorough list of the actions and steps you must take to accomplish your goals. Creating an action plan can help you stay motivated, focused, and organized as you work towards your goals. This is how to draft a successful action plan:

1. Break down your objective: Split your objective into more doable tasks or benchmarks. This facilitates achieving the objective and aids in your consistent advancement. If your objective is to complete a marathon in six months, you may divide it into smaller goals like running a longer distance each week, picking up a faster pace, or entering shorter races.

2. Set job priorities: Establish a task list based on their importance or timeliness. This might

assist you in concentrating on the activities that will most significantly affect how close you are to achieving your objective.

3. Establish deadlines: Give each task or milestone a deadline to foster a sense of urgency and help you stay on course. Ensure your deadlines are reasonable and doable, accounting for your time and other obligations.

4. Identify resources and support: Establish what equipment, resources, or assistance you need to finish each activity. Books, online classes, mentors, and specialized tools and equipment may all fall under this category. By being aware of these resources beforehand, you can reduce obstacles and remain organized.

5. How are you doing with each assignment or goal? This might support you in maintaining your motivation and modifying your action plan as needed if you encounter difficulties.

6. Modify your strategy as necessary: Be ready to alter your action plan if your situation

changes, you run into unforeseen difficulties, or you discover more efficient ways to accomplish your objective. Success requires both adaptability and flexibility.

7. Honour accomplishments: As you finish projects and reach goals, give yourself a pat for your efforts. This can support you in staying motivated and gaining momentum towards your objective.

Developing and adhering to a well-organized action plan can improve your chances of reaching your SMART objectives. As you work towards your goals, an action plan will help you keep organized and motivated by providing a clear roadmap.

Assignment of Tasks

One of the best ways to boost productivity and save time is to delegate chores. By assigning responsibilities, you free up your time to concentrate on higher-priority or more significant activities while others handle the lesser ones.

This chapter will cover the advantages of work delegation and practical methods.

1. Task delegation advantages: There are several advantages to task delegation, such as:
• Time savings: When you delegate assignments, you can devote more attention to higher-priority or more significant projects.
• Enhanced productivity: You can do more work in less time when you assign assignments to others, which raises overall productivity.

- Better teamwork: Assigning responsibilities to team members can promote improved communication, cooperation, and trust-building.
- Skill development: Assigning work to team members can aid in the growth of new or current skills.

2. Techniques for assigning work effectively: Clear communication, trust, and readiness to cede power are necessary for effective delegation. The following techniques can help you assign jobs more successfully:

- Clearly state the task and let the person completing it know what is expected of them.
- Select the correct individual: When assigning assignments, consider the recipient's qualifications, experience, and workload. Make

sure the person you select is qualified to finish the assignment.

- Provide resources: Ensure the individual can access the materials and knowledge required to finish the assignment.
- Establish a deadline: Give the individual finishing the assignment a precise timeframe that is both reasonable and understood.
- Check in frequently: Make sure the work is moving forward according to plan, offer input, and respond to inquiries by checking in frequently.
- This promotes future delegation and helps to establish confidence.

You may boost teamwork, increase productivity, and save time by distributing duties well.

The following section will discuss time blocking and how it can improve your task management.

Section Three

The Trap of Procrastination: How it Delays Your Goals

Though it's sometimes dismissed as a harmless habit, procrastination has a seductive quality that creeps into every part of our lives. Apart from the apparent setbacks in work, a complex network exists that entangles us, hinders our personal development, undermines professional accomplishments, and strains our relationships, ultimately diminishing our enjoyment and reducing our opportunities. This chapter delves deeply into the procrastination trap, examining its complex effects and revealing how it keeps us from realising our greatest potential.

Personal Development Halted

The root cause of the procrastination trap is a sneaky personal development stall. Procrastination is a vicious circle that prevents us from reaching our goals and puts out the spark of ambition before it can lead to significant advancement. When we develop the bad habit of putting off things that help us become better versions of ourselves, we hinder our progress and lose chances to pick up, understand, and use new abilities. Deliberate practice, or the consistent work put out to acquire abilities and reach mastery, is the fundamental idea of personal development. But procrastination undermines this habit, trapping us in a never-ending state of mediocrity. We forfeit the advancement that might propel us to greatness when we give in to the lure of rapid gratification, whether it takes the shape of amusement or distraction.

Harm to One's Career Prospects

Procrastination can have far-reaching effects on one's career and profession, potentially altering one's trajectory towards success. The ability to fulfil deadlines and consistently provide high-quality work are the cornerstones of job progress. These foundations are upset when we procrastinate excessively, which leads to poor work submissions, missed deadlines, and diminished credibility. Furthermore, the image of ineptitude that results from procrastinating might damage our reputation in the workplace. Our supervisors and coworkers might think less of us and doubt our capacity to handle significant tasks. This breakdown of trust can impede our ability to advance inside an organisation and restrict our options for professional advancement.

Personal Connections

Relationships are affected by procrastination in ways that go beyond its impact on our careers. Healthy relationships are undermined when we develop a pattern of putting off obligations, violating pledges, or avoiding accountability. It could become harder for friends, family, and coworkers to rely on us, which would cause dissatisfaction, disappointment, and strained relationships. Furthermore, delay carries an emotional cost that permeates our relationships. Unfinished business can cause stress, guilt, and anxiety, making us aloof, impatient, and less sensitive. In addition to isolating us from other people, the cycle of procrastination prevents us from forming meaningful relationships because it keeps us preoccupied with our conflicts.

Decline in Health

The psychological effects of procrastination are detrimental to our general well-being and put a pall over our mental and emotional well-being. Chronic stress results from unrelenting worry about approaching deadlines, remorse about leaving things undone, and the weight of unfinished business. Prolonged stress can worsen pre-existing mental health issues, cause burnout, and interfere with our ability to sleep. Moreover, procrastination amplifies our critical and negative self-talk. Our sense of value and self-esteem are damaged by the guilt and shame that come with avoidance, which serves to reinforce the idea that we are unworthy. Self-doubt and self-condemnation increase in the inner conversation, prolonging the procrastination cycle and intensifying our psychological pain.

Missed Chances

With its seductive charm, procrastination snatches chances that might not present themselves again. Whether it's an opportunity to pursue a passion project, an urgent investment, or a job offer that needs to be accepted right now, our propensity to put things off can cause us to lose out on possibilities that have a big impact on our lives. We unintentionally block pathways to a brighter future when prioritising convenience over long-term benefits. The temptation of procrastination causes us to lose sight of possibilities outside our comfort zones. Our focus moves from the possible benefits of the future to the fleeting comforts of the present when we break the cycle of procrastination. Because of this myopia, we cannot fully take advantage of the opportunities life presents us.

Encourage Bad Behaviour

Not only is procrastination a behaviour, but it's also a habit that can get stronger with time. Our brains become accustomed to delaying tasks and establishing strong connections between them and our neural pathways when we do so regularly. These brain pathways become more deeply ingrained as we give in to the comfort of avoidance and the desire for rapid fulfilment. This kind of brain adaptation can also apply to other aspects of our lives, leading to a vicious cycle of delay and inaction. Even when it goes against our long-term objectives, we are trained to choose the path of least resistance. This pattern eventually erodes our self-control and makes it harder for us to concentrate on important work.

c. Playing the underdog and giving it your all

Expectations place a lot of pressure on competitors. The hare was the clear favourite in popularity and skill, so the tortoise had nothing to lose. There's no pressure when there's nothing to lose. The tortoise ultimately just performed what it could do best.

This also makes me think of a proverb from the revered Indian book Bhagavad Gita: "Do your duty, but do not worry about the results." One can never control the outcome. Numerous known and unknown aspects are beyond our control or very little. Therefore, focusing our energy on our actions and cognitive processes is wiser than on external factors beyond our control.

Sometimes, the potential is outweighed by the weight of expectations. Even great athletes might falter from time to time under the pressure of expectations. It's difficult to overcome the fear of failing. When well controlled, it can become a driving force but occasionally completely paralyse us.

Regarding this matter, Mark H. McCormack wrote in his book, What Harvard Business School Doesn't Teach You: In the early summer of 1976, French Olympic hurdler Guy Drug found himself in a precarious situation, according to notes from a street-smart executive. As the sole prospect for a track and field medal in France, he began feeling the weight of the national pride bearing down on him. Subsequently, Drug informed me that he had spoken with our longstanding client, Jean-Claude Killy, multiple times before the games and that he genuinely believed Killy deserved a portion of Drug's gold medal. "Jean-Claude told me that I was the only one who knew how to get my body and mind to their ultimate peak for the Olympic Games," he said in his explanation. He then advised me to keep telling myself, "I have done everything I can to prepare for this race, and if I win, everything will be great, but if I don't win, Before the qualifying heats and during the interval between the semi-finals and finals, I told myself this same thing. I repeated the line repeatedly, which made all the other noises disappear. Even as I went up to pick up my gold medal, I was still saying it to myself.

5. The Mouse and the Lion

The inventiveness of this tale sets it apart. Aesop's Fable (number 150 in the Perry Index) is the story that follows. Interestingly, how a lion reacts to a mouse playing with it sounds so real that it feels more like a true story than a made-up event. In other versions of this tale, the lion is occasionally replaced by a herd of elephants.

Once, a little mouse snuck into the den of a lion. The lion slumbered soundly. The small mouse hopped up on the lion's tail, ran across its back, slid down its leg, and leapt off its paw while admiring the animal's massive mane and whiskers. The lion snapped the mouse between its paws as soon as it woke.

The mouse begged the lion to release it and assured him it would one day assist the lion in return.

The lion had to hold its belly, laughing so hard after hearing this! At once, the mouse bolted for cover.

After a few days, two hunters entered the forest and constructed a massive rope snare to capture the large lion. The lion entered the snare and became trapped while travelling to its den.

The powerful lion roared in pain as it struggled mightily to free itself. The same little mouse just so happened to be passing by and heard the pathetic roar; it raced to find out what had happened. It observed that the lion was caught in a snare made of rope.

The mouse examined the trap and saw it was all held together by a single, thick rope. It began nibbling until the rope broke. At last, the lion was free after shaking off the other ropes holding him in place.

The lion turned to the mouse in joy and thanked it for the saving gesture despite ridiculing it for its size earlier.

Monitor Your Development And Honour Victories

And lastly, remember to enjoy your accomplishments! Reward yourself for your achievements when you progress towards your goals. Honouring minor victories inspires you and reaffirms that your efforts have been worthwhile.

Determine the benchmarks or incentives that will keep you on course. This could be as easy as giving yourself a nice treat after finishing a task on schedule. Or even a day off whenever you accomplish a particular degree of achievement. Maintaining a progress log and acknowledging your accomplishments will help you stay motivated and focused.

Bonus Step 9: Honour Your Achievements!

Ultimately, it's critical to acknowledge the triumphs and accomplishments encountered along the route. Make sure you take time to celebrate when you do anything, like following a schedule for two days or finishing all of your assignments on time! This will support your motivation and remind you that effort is rewarded.

Although it's not a simple task, it is possible to break the habit of being late with commitment and perseverance. By remaining organized and establishing realistic goals, you can
It can be difficult to make changes in life, but it's crucial to maintain your optimism and remember that anything is achievable with perseverance. It's not impossible to break the habit of being late. If you follow the advice in this post, you should have no trouble succeeding! Wishing you luck!

Practice: Reduce Outside Distractions

Another key strategy for helping persons with ADHD manage distractions is to minimize outside distractions, such as noise, visual stimuli, and other people's disruptions. The following techniques can help reduce outside distractions:

● Diminish noise: Shut windows and doors, use noise-cancelling headphones, or find a quieter place.

● Eliminate visual disturbances: Reduce the amount of open tabs or windows on your computer, clear the clutter off your workstation, and turn off notifications on your phone and computer.

● Interact with others: Inform friends, family, and coworkers when you need to concentrate and politely request that they not bother you during that period.

- Establish limits: To reduce outside distractions, set up a specific workstation and defined work hours.
- Take regular breaks: To prevent mental tiredness and help your brain recover, give yourself regular rest. When you go back to work, this can help you maintain your attention.

The Paradox of Perfectionism

For those with ADHD, perfectionism and distractibility are frequently related. Overly focusing on details due to perfectionism can make staying focused and avoiding distractions challenging. It is simple to become mired in when you are preoccupied with perfecting everything. This may result in analysis paralysis, in which you spend so much time dissecting every facet of a task that you cannot move forward.

Target when you're easily distracted. This may cause you to worry that you won't finish tasks since you were preoccupied with something else and couldn't focus fully on it. Distractions can also feed perfectionism and the ensuing dread of making mistakes.

If you have ADHD, you may already be acquainted with the experience of falling short of expectations—whether they be your own or those of others. This fear may be so strong that it prevents you from beginning an activity or undertaking. Procrastination can result from this, as you put off beginning because you're afraid you won't do it right.

Changing your attention from results to processes is crucial if you want to overcome perfectionism. Pay more attention to the steps you must take to get there rather than the outcome. Divide the work into smaller, more manageable phases, and give each one a reasonable aim. This can assist you in maintaining process focus and preventing you from becoming bogged down by the wider picture.

Furthermore, it's critical to give oneself permission to make errors and grow from them. Rigid thinking, where mistakes are viewed as failures rather than opportunities for improvement, is frequently the result of perfectionism. Improvement and learning. You may become less fearful of making mistakes and feel more confident, which can increase your productivity and help you move your work along more quickly.

Recall that the secret to success is not perfection but rather development. Instead of concentrating only on the outcome, recognize your efforts and celebrate your small victories. You can escape the loop of perfectionism and diversion and work towards more achievement and fulfilment by concentrating on your progress.

Use a productivity tool or app to keep motivated and track your progress.

It might feel like an uphill battle to retain productivity and manage time effectively as we traverse the complexities of today's fast-paced digital environment. Employing a productivity tool or app has become a well-liked and successful strategy among the many approaches to increase productivity. Using technology, we may improve our productivity and effectiveness by streamlining our workflow, being organized, and keeping motivated.

A platform made to assist individuals or groups in completing work more quickly and successfully. Including communication, time monitoring, project planning, and task management. These apps can greatly lessen the cognitive load associated with multitasking and task-switching, freeing up mental resources for more concentrated work by offering an orderly and centralized platform to handle tasks.

Productivity apps have the potential to revolutionize the task management industry. These programmes let you make, organize, rank, and manage projects so you can see a clear picture of how much work you have on your hands. Doing this lets you maintain your organization, use your time wisely, and keep things from becoming neglected. Furthermore, because these applications give you a clear picture of your work and its status, you can see the fruits of your labour and stay motivated.

Time monitoring features can also be found in productivity apps. By better understanding how you're using your time, these features can help you spot trends, bottlenecks, and areas where you can make improvements. For example, you may find that some tasks are taking longer than anticipated or that you are devoting an excessive amount of time to less critical tasks. By offering this insight, time tracking can facilitate better informed and efficient decision-making regarding work prioritization and time management.

Many productivity apps include teamwork and communication tools, time monitoring, and task management. Teams may particularly benefit from this since it facilitates coordinated task management, centralized information, and efficient communication. These applications can increase team cohesion and efficiency by fostering better communication and cooperation.

Even if there are many advantages to productivity applications, selecting one based on your unique requirements, working style, and preferences is crucial. Several variables, such as the type of work you do, the size of your team, your preferred working style, and your personal preferences, will determine which productivity tool is best for you. While choosing one, consider an app's features, user interface, usability, tool integrations, and customer service.

Moreover, productivity applications are not a panacea, even though they can greatly increase productivity. Dedicated work habits and a dedication to productivity are necessary to effectively use these technologies. Using productivity apps in conjunction with other productivity tactics, like time management methods, scheduled breaks, and preserving a positive work-life balance is critical.

To sum up, productivity applications can be an effective weapon in your toolbox for increasing productivity. These technologies can boost productivity by offering a centralized and well-organized platform for managing work, tracking time, and facilitating communication. They can also keep users motivated and increase efficiency. But it's crucial to keep in mind that they are only instruments. Their efficacy depends on how they are applied; for optimum results, they should be utilized in conjunction with productive work practices and habits.

Benefits Of Effective Time Management.

Effective time management benefits both the company and its employees. Among these benefits are the following:

Increased worker happiness. Employees are happier and less likely to experience burnout when they have enough time to complete their tasks.

A rise in originality. Employees can be more innovative when time constraints do not constrain them. People might actively engage with them instead of just reacting passively to their jobs. This promotes creativity.

● A reduction in absences. Take more time off for illness.

Decreased attrition. Better work experience increases the likelihood of sticking to one job rather than looking for another.

Enhanced efficiency. Employees who enjoy their work and have lower absenteeism rates are more productive.

A better standing. Businesses that encourage efficient time management are desirable workplaces, improving employee attraction and retention.

Additional benefits of effective time management include ● Reduction of stress.

Anxiety is reduced when a work plan is made and followed. You may tell that you are moving closer to your goals when you cross things off of your "to-do" list. This keeps you from being anxious and worried about whether you're doing tasks.

● More time

You may spend more time in your daily life when you manage your time well. Those who are good at managing their time value having more time for hobbies and other personal activities.

- Additional chances

When time is managed well, opportunities increase, and less time is wasted on unimportant tasks. Proficient time management skills are essential competencies that employers look for. Planning and prioritising tasks is extremely beneficial for any kind of organisation.

Capacity to achieve objectives

Individuals who have good time management skills.

You, the workplace, and procrastination

At work, procrastination is an issue. In addition to stress, anxiety, and sadness, it can result in reduced performance and low productivity. Additionally, procrastination might result in health issues like heart disease or elevated blood pressure. Procrastination has far-reaching consequences on your physical health, how you feel about yourself, and how others see you. These repercussions go far beyond your personal life.

Not only do people who procrastinate work that must be done, but they also put their health at risk by delaying sleep for an additional hour of Netflix viewing or worse at night.

Let procrastination be your time thief. It is a widespread issue that impacts individuals from various backgrounds and stages of life. It occurs so frequently that we have a global term: "yuck." This is the same word you'd use to describe something repulsive or unsightly.

The causes of procrastination are as different as those who indulge in this behaviour. These consist of ● Fear (such as What if I fail?) ● Laziness (such as I don't want to do this).

Interruptions (such as reminding oneself to check email!)

There are numerous causes of procrastination.

There are numerous causes of procrastination. These are a few of the most typical ones:

- Absence of drive (and self-control)
- Inadequate time management abilities
- Inattention and disorganisation in planning and preparation
- Insufficient energy, drive, and self-control

Things go wrong when we put things off.

Let procrastination be your time thief. It deprives you of the here and now and prevents you from reaching your full potential. Things go wrong when we put things off. Because we believe we will never catch up, it leads to stress, anxiety, and concern. Furthermore, completing a project or assignment can be so stressful that we fail to appreciate our accomplishments or look forward to taking on new tasks as a result. The greatest strategy to beat procrastination is to work towards your objective gradually each day until it becomes ingrained in your routine.

Ignorance is a weak justification for putting off tasks that must be completed.

● Putting off tasks is a weak justification for procrastination. ● A time thief is procrastination.

It's time to get things done and quit making excuses!

Anything worthwhile to accomplish is worthwhile to do well.

It won't take long for something to stop being a priority in your life if you don't take the time to do it correctly. Your focus and efforts will shift, leaving behind a disorganised heap of unfinished projects, hesitant endeavours, and guilt trails that follow us everywhere we go—even into our dreams. Learn to identify your priorities and set aside time for them every day—one hour on the weekdays, two hours on the weekends, or whatever works best for you—to escape this fate!

Regain control over your procrastination and complete the tasks at hand.

To take charge of your life, you must first recognise the issue. Are you still holding out for the one item that would solve everything? Are you waiting for instructions from someone else?

How can procrastination be recognised? When someone starts something but doesn't finish it, that person is procrastinating. They lack motivation since they are not committed, which prevents them from acting.

Since procrastinators frequently experience high-stress levels, they might believe taking a break would enable them to unwind and reduce their tension. This is counterproductive, though, as procrastination can become an addiction that keeps people from completing tasks that are truly important to them or that they truly want to do (like finishing their homework). Put another way, when we procrastinate, we remain inside our comfort zones rather than venturing outside, where we can discover exciting surprises!

Irregular timing leads to tension.

Delaying things might cause tension. Your thoughts won't be clear if you try to concentrate on anything and keep putting it off. You'll take longer to complete tasks, which will eventually cause you to become more stressed. The longer this cycle goes on, the more difficult it is for your brain to get out of its rut and begin functioning normally.

Procrastination-related stress is bad for your health as well. Stress has been connected to several illnesses, including diabetes and heart disease. Still, it can also aggravate other bodily issues, such as headaches or stomachaches, by gradually lowering immunity.

With all these bad feelings, you can even be nervous about starting your task! Nothing is worse than being aware that crucial tasks need to be completed but being overcome with panic every time those tasks aren't completed immediately or at all. This makes sense when we consider how our brains are wired: they are made to help us feel good when we do things we enjoy (like watching T.V.), but not so much when we do things that aren't enjoyable but still require our attention (like doing the dishes). This is one of the reasons why some people find it more difficult than others to overcome their procrastinating tendencies; they could find themselves torn between two equally unpleasant options: either putting up with their obligations while feeling miserable about them OR ignoring them completely and feeling bad about it later on when they have to face the consequences of their decisions because of what went wrong the last time.

Which five elements make up goal-setting?

The fundamental goal requirements are S.M.A.R.T. objectives, which are specific, measurable, achievable, relevant, and time-bound. These five standards ensure the goals are relevant and centre around the team members and the business's overall professional development.

Particular

Any goal that requires development needs to have a clear destination. Whether the objective is to launch a new product, boost sales, or soothe customer concerns, being as specific as possible about the target improves project planning and execution.

Quantifiable

It's not always feasible to quantify results or even precise objectives. Managers and leaders must start over and establish a new goal if this is the case. If results are significantly below expectations, managers and other leaders can intervene. Teams can utilise a progress monitoring strategy to determine whether they are headed in the right direction.

Realistic

When reasonable but slightly unachievable goals are maintained, workers stay focused and support the development of their talents.

Producing ten thousand audio cassettes daily is a specific, measurable, and achievable goal, but is it relevant? Set goals and monitor metrics to keep staff members engaged, but little progress will be achieved. Focusing on pertinent goals is the greatest. Companies need to be on the lookout for Fotoday's approaches to stay innovative.

Time-limited

Wishes are all that ambitious goals with no deadline are. Managers and team members will most likely put off accomplishing the goals if there is no deadline.

Purposeful goals are the foundation of effective ones. The ability of managers to set objectives and associated benchmarks aids teams tremendously in locating possible bottlenecks, capitalising on momentum, and accomplishing the intended result. They want to help managers make plans, not just wish and fantasise.

Setting Goals Is Crucial For Any Organisation.

As organisations become closer to adopting a hybrid working style, managers are more responsible for giving their team members the greatest support available. Daily tasks performed by employees and supervisors can effectively incorporate this "monitored autonomy" with the help of comprehensive goal planning that considers important outcomes and tracking technologies. Managers can set realistic expectations and give their staff the freedom to succeed by creating S.M.A.R.T. goals. Well-known businesses like Microsoft and Google are putting into practice plans based on concepts covered in Dan Pink's Ted Talk regarding the significance of autonomy for motivation. These companies aim to give employees greater control over their tasks, responsibilities, and goals.

In addition to offering clarity and motivation, employee goals help employees complete their work more successfully. If project staff members know their goals, studies show that when creating staff goals, it is critical to ensure that all involved are dedicated to reaching them and actively desire to do so. Managers and leaders can help by getting a sense of what is meaningful, satisfying, or compatible with the personal beliefs of their staff members. According to a Deloitte survey, an increasing proportion of millennial employees recognise their value in the workplace and are committed to upholding the company's mission and values.

The six approaches to goal-setting in organisations

One of the most significant duties of managers and human resource departments is goal-setting. To help employees comprehend key results and business objectives, management, human resources, and the workforce collaborate to develop company goals, policies, and procedures. Establishing attainable goals improves employee engagement, which increases the chance that staff members will flourish.

Human resource managers should consider these six tried-and-true tactics when setting goals for their team members.

Utilising the Trust Dimensions in a Workplace

Managing people, not only tasks, is your main duty as a manager. It is crucial to realise that your staff members are more than just resources that should be used on various tasks. They are aspirational, goal-oriented, emotional human beings. Being a good leader means showing people that you care about their welfare, both at work and outside.

Holding one-on-one meetings with your staff regularly is one approach to show that you care. These discussions ought to cover more than just work-related topics. Talks about their personal life, aspirations, and professional objectives should also be included. Spend time getting to know them, asking open-ended questions, and demonstrating your sincere interest in their life.

Demonstrating an interest in your colleagues' personal lives may foster a more relaxed and transparent work environment that increases employee trust and loyalty. This can also assist you in determining areas in which they might require more resources or assistance, such as flexible work schedules or mental health services.

Talking with your staff about their career aspirations shows them you care about their growth and future. In addition to inspiring them to give their best work, this can assist you in identifying possible areas for internal growth or career advancement.

ACT NOW: Plan on checking in with your direct reports regularly. Make a Google Doc for running notes to which you can add agenda items.

Your team needs to normalise providing and accepting feedback. You must regularly and in various ways ask your employees for input to achieve this.

www.ingramcontent.com/pod-product-compliance
Lightning Source LLC
Chambersburg PA
CBHW052150110526
44591CB00012B/1920